POTTY TRAINING A PUPPY

by Ethan Adrian

:

BOOK DESCRIPTION

Potty training a pup can often turn out to be a tough task. It might sometimes seem like a simple work but at the end turn out to be annoying and frustrating if done wrongly.

With little know how you will end up wasting a lot of energy and time resulting to frustrations. The Main goal of this book is to simplify and enlighten any new owner to potty training. In addition, add more knowledge to all pup owners on how to effective potty train a puppy. The book will solve all common problems you may go through during the potty training process.

Without proper potty training tricks and techniques, it may be difficult for a puppy to learn how to potty effectively. This book will showcase the best ways to train your puppy well. Remember, patience is a significant factor to consider while potty training your puppy.

As a pup owner, you expect the dog to bring a lot of happiness in the home but without the essential potty training techniques, it's going to be a bad experience between you and the puppy. Get rid of all bad experience by making this book your teacher.

Contents

INTRODUCTION

One of the biggest reasons puppies and dogs end up in shelters is because the owner has not been successful in-house training them. House training a puppy or dog is vital to your relationship, and it will ensure the two of you have a long and happy life together, free from the stress of messes in the house. The appropriate time to start potty training is as soon as you get your puppy because once a dog thinks it's okay for him to relieve himself in the house, it will become a difficult behavior to break.

As the owner, it's your responsibility to teach your puppy to mess outside. Puppies do not come equipped with this knowledge. If your puppy messes in the house, consider it your fault. You weren't watching him close enough! If he messes in his crate, consider that your fault as well! You left him in his crate too long. This may sound harsh but many problems could easily be avoided if puppies were better understood.

Before you bring your puppy home you need to be fully committed to the raising and training of your puppy. If you already have your puppy then you need to decide right now if you will commit yourself to properly train it. It takes time, patience, understanding, and persistence to train a well-behaved family companion. But, I guarantee your hard work now will pay off with years of loving companionship.

Much like children you need to teach your puppy where and when it is acceptable to go to the bathroom. At the age of 12 weeks, puppies have little or no control over when and where they go. If your puppy is four months old they'll be able to wait around 4 hours to go potty. At night, by four months, your puppy should be able to hold it overnight. Establish a regular feeding schedule alongside your puppy out time and potty breaks.

When outside, try to take your puppy to a certain spot to go to the bathroom, this helps it associate inside and outside. Don't forget to praise your puppy when it does go potty in the right spot.

CHAPTER 1

TIPS TO SUCCEED IN POTTY TRAINING

These are a few key tips that will help you achieve the desired behavior from your puppy when potty training him.

- ✓ **Maintain realistic expectations** - Even well-behaved puppies can be unpredictable on occasion. You're dealing with a very young dog, and changing behavior will take weeks and even months.

- ✓ **Remember affection works** - Puppies want to be loved, pet and rewarded. When you respond to positive behaviors with a lot of love, you have a much better chance of training your dog to behave. If you don't want your dog messing in the house, lead him outside to do his business. When he does it right and at the right spot, give him a treat and praise him.

- ✓ **Pay attention to your dog** - Not all puppies are exactly alike. They are unique, with different personalities and traits. What works for one puppy might not work for all puppies. The first few weeks that you spend with your puppy should tell you how he responds to certain commands, consequences, and rewards. Instead of working against the puppy's natural instincts, work with them. It's important to train a puppy not to mess in the house rather ring the puppy doorbell or bark when he wants to go out to potty.

But you want the dog to have the freedom to bark when there is the danger, so it's important to balance behavior modification with remembering that a dog is going to be a dog. If your puppy barks excessively, don't get mad at or shout at him. The dog may get the impression that you too are joining in. Consistently say "**quiet**" in a firm and calm voice when you want him to stop barking. After he stops barking, take him out to potty and reward him with praise and a treat.

✓ **Keep your commands clear** - Tell your puppy exactly what you want. Saying "**no**" is a command, but if you want the puppy to do something beyond that, you need to be specific. Get a puppy to sit or lie down by physically pointing to or patting a spot where the dog should rest and remain. You don't want to confuse your puppy and if you're just yelling all the time, it's not going to dissuade bad behavior.

✓ **Maintain consistency** - Dogs learn from repetition. You'll need to practice behavior training with your puppy on a regular basis. Teach them to go outside when they need to potty. If the puppy relieves himself in the house, don't get mad at him. Rather, clean the mess and continue with the potty training schedule until the puppy gets that it is appropriate to only potty outside.

✓ **Reinforce good behavior** - You aren't going to get the behavior you want from your puppy unless you reinforce it. Use treats liberally while training your puppy because they work. Playing outside, taking walks and just cuddling on the couch are other positive reinforcements that will work with your dog. Don't hand out treats for no reason. Give them to your puppy specifically after a good behavior is produced. When the dog stops messing in the house and goes outside to potty, reward that dog with a treat. It might seem like bribery, but that's okay. Your goal is to do what works.

Once your puppy has reached the right age, it's important to establish a potty training routine and to be consistent and patient with it. You will need to take your puppy out immediately after he wakes up, 15 minutes after he eats or drinks, at least once an hour while he is awake before you put him in his crate and immediately after you take him out of the crate. To help prevent accidents, be sure you keep your puppy on a regular feeding schedule and remove the food once he has finished eating, but always allow him access to water. Puppy's digestive systems are quick and efficient and taking him out 15 minutes after he eats will help get him used to go potty outside.

Puppies cannot be expected to hold their bladders all night, so you will also need to set an alarm during the night so you can take him outside. Expecting your puppy to hold his bladder throughout the night is not only unrealistic, it is a sure fire way to ensure he soils his crate or gets a nasty bladder infection trying to hold it far longer than he is capable of or should be expected. It is also important to watch for the bathroom **"tells"** puppies often display. Twirling in circles, whining, scratching and sniffing the floor are often indications the puppy needs to potty, so if you see or hear these things, take him outside immediately.

It is also important that you take your puppy to the same spot every time to use the bathroom. Be patient with your puppy, do not try to force him, yell at him or rush him to use the potty. Simply stand in the designated spot and use upbeat, positive verbal encouragements to **"go potty"** and allow your puppy time to sniff out the perfect spot and do his business. Once your puppy does his business, be sure to reward him with positive praise, a treat and lots of snuggles, pets, and kisses. Make it a rewarding, happy experience so your dog feels good when he sees you get the leash and say the words **"go potty**." Most puppies truly want to please their masters and letting your puppy know he is good and did the right thing will help your puppy's potty training progress at a faster rate.

HOW TO EFFECTIVE POTTY TRAIN A PUP

- ✓ **Journal keeping** – When potty training a pup, it is crucial that you understand how commonly your pup has to relieve himself. If your dog's routine is stable, he will normally have a constant washroom regimen. Tape-record exactly what time they went and what business they did. Determine how long they are holding it. That is your standard. It is necessary during this time that you feed your dog on a routine. Do not leave the bowl of kibble on the ground, or it will be difficult to predict accidents.

- ✓ **Crate** – a crate is a helpful tool when it comes to potty training a pup. Now that you have actually established a baseline with your journal, you know how long your dog can hold it.

- ✓ **Taking him out** - When you are house-training your dog, you must always go outside with him to see that he goes. Walk him (don't hold him) out the door you at some point desire him to use to alert you. This will build a routine. Once he does his business, wait a few more minutes. Many puppies will go again virtually instantly. You will learn your new puppy's regular. Any time he does his business outside, praise him and offers him a treat or fun game.

✓ **Create a routine** – After a successful first step in potty training pup, it is time to repeat the same after a scheduled period of time. Take him outside and await him to do the proper business. If he does, give him a reward and allow him house freedom.

✓ **Learn how to handle and prevent accidents** - Your dog must never be running free in the house without you. If you cannot supervise, put him in his pet crate. You can't penalize for mishaps after the truth because canines don't discover that way. If you see him start to show the indications, such as smelling, turning in a circle or squatting, start clapping your hands and rush him out the marked door. Do not get upset, simply act urgently. As soon as he gets outside, rewards him for going.

The key thing to pup potty training is consistency. With the few tricks and techniques above, your pup will house break in just a short period of time.

CHAPTER 2

POTTY TRAINING

The most effective method to achieve quality results in potty training your puppy is using the clicker. **Clicker training** is a training method which relies on positive reinforcement, rather than coercion or correction, and uses the principles of both classical conditioning and operant conditioning. The Clicker Potty Training Method is designed for puppies and dogs of all breeds, ages, and sizes. **This method will work** no matter what your schedule is, provided you follow the guidelines. Before you begin this or any potty training method, keep in mind that young puppies just aren't capable of holding it for extended periods of time. Once they are anywhere from 3-5 months old they should be able to hold it for longer periods. Consult your vet if you feel your puppy is going way too much or not enough because some potty training problems are caused by the puppy or dog being ill.

Don't expect too much from your puppy either. He's a puppy and will do what comes naturally or what was unintentionally taught to him. It's your job to teach him what is and isn't acceptable behavior. Don't slack off because you feel your puppy is stupid and incapable of learning or because you've just had it with trying to teach him to go outside for three weeks and he's still messing in the house. All puppies can and will learn if given the proper instruction and time to learn. So get ready to begin properly potty training your puppy! Before we begin, take note of these potty training steps:

- ✓ Ensure that you take your puppy out when he wakes up, after eating and drinking, when you first get home, and after play sessions.

- ✓ Take him outside through the same door.

- ✓ Take him to the same spot.

- ✓ Bring him back in through the same door.

- ✓ Take your puppy out on a leash.

- ✓ Clean up messes inside with a solution of half vinegar and half water.

- ✓ Choose a phrase as his **"Go potty"** signal and use it as soon as you get him to his spot.

- ✓ Leave a few stools at his bathroom area.

- ✓ Rush your puppy outside if he starts to mess in the house.

- ✓ Keep him on a set schedule for feeding, walking.

- ✓ Learn not to rub your puppy's nose in his mess.

- ✓ Make sure you don't leave him in his crate for longer periods than he can handle.

- ✓ Avoid scolding or hitting him for making a mess in the house.

- ✓ Avoid playing with him before he goes to the bathroom.

✓ Don't allow let him run around the house before he's fully trustworthy.

✓ Avoid the use of newspaper when potty training. They're messy and confuse your pup.

✓ Make sure you do not use different doors to take him outside and back in.

✓ You should never ignore your puppy's need to go out no matter how tired you are.

This method is based on the popular clicker training for dogs. Instead of using the clicker for every aspect of training, you'll be using it for potty training only, thereby increasing its effectiveness. If you don't have a clicker, visit your nearest pet store. You should be able to get two of them for just a few dollars. Make sure you get two just in case you misplace or break one.

You can use this method whether you have a puppy or dog, work all day or are at home, or if you've already started a different potty training method and it hasn't worked. Simply throw out the other ideas you've had about potty training and start fresh. This method is so easy to teach and most puppies and dogs will catch on extremely quickly. Keep in mind though that **your puppy will need to have a good diet and a strict schedule**. No puppy will become potty trained if he is fed **"less than quality"** food and if he's fed whenever. You need to be completely dedicated, no matter how tired you are! Remember, a puppy learns only what he has been taught. Your puppy's good behavior, or lack of, reflects directly on you! Before you begin with this method you need to set your puppy up for success.

Since your puppy is young, chances are he simply can't hold it for more than a few hours at a time. It would be very cruel of us to expect him to hold it all day so be prepared to clean up messes until he's around 3-5 months of age. To help control where he messes in the house you will need to set up a room, an exercise pen, or a large crate. Any of these three will be large enough for him to have areas to play, sleep, and mess. If we don't give him room to do these things he will probably develop the nasty habit of messing where he sleeps. This is a very difficult habit to break so let's prevent it from ever happening. If you use a room or exercise pen I suggest having a crate available for him to sleep in. This will prepare him for when he's older and you want to crate him when you leave.

When you set up the area he will use when alone, be sure he has something comfortable to sleep on, and the material you want him to normally mess on outside. If you want him to always go on the grass, place a piece of sod in his area. One piece should last nearly a week if you just clean up the poop. You want to leave the urine smell in the sod since this will attract your puppy back to the sod. If you prefer he always go on the cement outside, get a thin slab of cement for his area. Again, **just clean off the poop** and every few days rinse the slab with plain water. It is inappropriate to cover the floor with newspapers since this gets very messy and it teaches him to use any newspaper as his toilet. You'll also want to make sure he has some good toys to play with. You can also place a small dish of water in his area.

Now we're ready to begin! If you haven't brought your puppy home yet plan on starting this from the second you pick him up. If you already have your pup, start this when you'll have a few full days to work on it. First, we need to associate the clicker with something very good. There is no better reward for a puppy than a **tasty treat** when training.

And what behavior other than going to the bathroom outside deserves something this good? Grab your puppy, the clicker, and a few treats you know your puppy likes. It will work better if you do this outside on the surface you want him to use, at his designated potty spot, since you'll always be clicking and treating his behavior outside.

All you need to do now is **click a few times** then give him a treat. Choose how many times you'll click the clicker so he knows what he's doing well every time. Once or twice should do. Be sure to only give him a small piece of the treat. Don't give him a whole mouthful. Continue to click and treat every few minutes. Once he hears the clicks and looks to you for a treat you know he's caught on. Now we wait until he goes to the bathroom. As soon as he starts to pee or poop click the clicker, however, many times you've decided on. When he's finished, give him a treat and **really praise him**. Put your clicker away until the next time you take him out to the bathroom. Repeat this every time he goes.

Once your puppy has had no accidents in the house for at least 2 weeks, it's time to start teaching him to let you know when he needs to go out. This will be addressed in the upcoming section, The Puppy Doorbell. After teaching him how to let you know he needs to go out, it's **time to start eliminating the clicker and treats**. This should only be started after at least two weeks of no accidents in the house and your pup letting you know consistently that he needs to go out.

We can now assume that your puppy understands that he is expected to go to the bathroom outside and that he'll let you know it, so it should be safe to begin! Start this on a weekend morning or anytime you'll have a few days to dedicate to this.

Take him out as you normally would in the morning. Click and treat as normal for this time. The next time you take him out, don't click but give a treat. Couple this with plenty of praise. Take him back in and wait until the next time he needs to go out. Click and treat for this one. Do the click and treat for every other bathroom break for the rest of the day. If he seems okay with everything and is still going to the door to be let out, with no accidents in the house, we can move on to the next day. If he backslides even one time with either not letting you know he needs to go out or going to the bathroom in the house, go back to click and treating every time. He obviously isn't ready. Give him a few more days and try again. If everything went smoothly your first day, click and treat every third bathroom break. Continue this for a few days and if all is well, try eliminating the click and treat altogether for one day. If he has accidents in the house go back a step.

If all goes well, **forget the click and treat** for a few days and monitor his behavior. If he seems okay with the new arrangement, pat yourself on the back! You now have a potty trained puppy!

If your puppy makes a mistake in the house, go back one step and continue working on that particular step for a few days. Some puppies may catch on to this right away and others may take weeks or even months. But I assure you that this method is by far easier to teach than any other method. Puppies just seem to understand what is expected of them better than strictly using a crate or exercise pen. Keep in mind that **you shouldn't use the clicker for any other training**. You don't want to confuse him.

You can alter this method to fit your needs for other potty training. If you want to train your pup to mess in a litter box, simply click every time he goes in it. Follow the same guidelines, with the exception of teaching him how to let you know he needs to go out. Or if you have a doggy door, you can teach this method with much quicker results. Set your pup's pen up in front of the doggy door when you're gone and he'll be potty trained in no time! First, you must teach him to go out the doggy door. This is a matter of simply coaxing him through it, while you hold it open, to get his dinner. Do this a few times until he seems okay with it. Then close the door and have someone coax him through to the other side. This shouldn't take much more than a few times. When teaching with the use of a doggy door keep in mind that you'll still need to go out with him to click and treat. Let him go out the doggy door and once he's through you simply go out behind him.

For Two Puppy Homes

Potty training using a clicker for more than one puppy can be **a little tricky**. You don't want one puppy to hear the click from outside and think he's done something good inside. This could very well turn out disastrous! At the same time, potty training could go much quicker. I assume you'll be taking both of the puppies outside at the same time? When one puppy goes, click and treat him. The other one will want a treat too so wait until he goes then click and treat him. **Puppies are very competitive** so once your pups catch on that they'll get a treat for going outside they'll be trying to go quicker than the other one so they get the treat first! If you're having trouble with them only wanting to play while they're supposed to be going to the bathroom, you'll have to take them out one after the other

Hopefully, each of their potty areas is in an area where the pup inside won't hear the clicker. Close the window if you think he'll hear. Once they catch on that going to the bathroom brings a click, which produces a treat, they'll be much more apt to go when taken out together. Make sure they each have their own bathroom area, too. It doesn't need to be on opposite sides of the yard but rather 5-10 feet apart.

The Puppy Doorbell

Everyone wants their puppy to notify them when he needs to go out. You'll have to decide how you want your pup to let you know. Most people don't want their pup jumping on the door or scratching at the door since this only creates damaged doors. The easiest method I've taught to date is **the puppy door bell**. You simply hang a bell from your doorknob, mount it on the wall at your pup's level, or use one of those bells that you hit the top and it dings (place this kind on the floor). Or you can use another method of teaching your puppy to bark when he needs to go out. I find this method much more difficult to teach since many puppies won't bark until they're older, and some breeds just aren't inclined to bark. I'm going to teach you how to teach your puppy to notify you of the use of a bell.

Before you can work on this, though, your puppy needs to know that messing is supposed to be done outside only. Your **puppy should be fully trustworthy** when you're home with him in the house. It works best at this time because your puppy knows he should go outside, but he just doesn't know how to get out. And at this time, he should be old enough to hold it for longer periods, allowing you to take him out at certain times without having to clean up any messes in the house.

Once you've got your bell in place, you'll need to show your puppy the bell. Encourage him to sniff it, lick it, whatever. If he happens to make it sound off open the door and take him out. If he doesn't make it sound off, you can do it, then open the door and take him out. I suggest having his leash on him when you practice with the bell so you have control of him when you take him out. Of course, every time he does something good be sure to praise him; whether he touches the bell, makes it sound off, looks at the door after making noise, anything. Be most lavish with your praise if he rings the bell then looks to the door.

Have him ring the bell every time before you go out and very soon he should catch on that ringing the bell opens the door which allows him to go to the bathroom. Be very vigilant about this and before too long you will hear the bell when you're watching television. This is the time when you really praise and let him know how good he is. Immediately take him outside to his spot.

CHAPTER 3

HOW TO HANDLE ACCIDENTS

Now you're probably wondering **how to handle it** when he goes on and messes in the house. Well, you do nothing but clean it up. Don't scold him, yell at him, and never hit him. You **should not punish the puppy** for having an accident. Often times, this is going to do more harm than it will do good, and it can damage the trust that the puppy has built up for you, causing it to fear you. Simply ensure that you clean the area, making sure that the scent of the urine or feces is completely gone. This is important because if the puppy smells the scent, he will go back to the same area over and over again. At no point should you rub the puppy's nose in the urine or feces, as this could cause the dog to become very sick.

Greet him like you always do. If he goes in the house when he's loose and with you, consider it your fault. You simply weren't watching him close enough! Provided you click and treat every time he goes to the bathroom outside he will catch on that good things happen when he goes outside but nothing happens when he goes in the house. Before long, he'll want to go outside all the time to go to the bathroom and get a treat.

By using a few days to get him used to his spot outside on the surface you've chosen, chances are he'll go on that same surface in the house. If he doesn't, try making his indoor mess area a little bigger or placing a small chunk of sod where he's previously gone pee on top of his indoor sod. Before long, you should have a puppy that willingly holds it until he can get outside. **Don't expect too much** from a puppy under 12-16 weeks old or a small breed puppy, though. Young and very small puppies just aren't physically capable of holding it that long.

It is important to keep an eye on the puppy when you are potty training him. Do not allow him to have access to the entire house because this will raise the chance of him soiling in a hidden area when he's out of your line of sight. Keep doors to bedrooms closed and use dog gates to keep your pup within your line of vision at all times. It's important to remember that even the smartest puppies don't have bladder control yet. **Puppies younger than 12 weeks old** can't be trained yet because they just don't have the capability. Young dogs also don't know how to tell you when they need to eliminate their waste. They may be aware of it, but they have not yet figured out how to tell you.

Accidents are going to happen. Just accept accidents as part of the process and do not overreact to them. There are going to be times when the puppy simply has an accident, even though you have taken him outside regularly. Your puppy is not being willful, disobedient or resistant, it's simply part of the process so do not punish him by spanking him, rubbing his nose in it or yelling at him. If you notice your pup is beginning to pee or poop in the house, clap your hands or make a loud noise. You want to startle the puppy and get its attention, but you don't want to scare the dog. Calmly say **"No"** and take him to his spot outside.

You can also make a loud noise with the intention of startling the dog. For example, saying loudly, "**Outside**," and then take the puppy straight to his potty spot, and allow him to finish there. **Praise him** with a treat when he'd done.

When an accident does occur in the house, simply clean up the accident and move on. You cannot apply a correction after the fact, the puppy will have no idea what is going on, why he is being told **"No"** or what it is he was supposed to do. If the puppy has frequent accidents, you might want to start taking it outside more often, because you do not want it to get confused and think it is okay for him to relieve himself inside of the house.

It is also **important for you to make plans** if you are going to be away from the house for a long period of time. It is very difficult for a person to house train a dog when they are at work 10 hours per day and the puppy is left alone all day. If this is going to be the case, have someone stay at your house, and **follow the puppy's schedule**.

Unlike humans, puppies live in the moment and once it has passed, they do not have a recollection of the accident and trying to discipline a puppy for a past action will only make him scared and make it difficult for him to trust you. Never, ever strike your puppy when you find accidents, or for any other reason. Hitting your puppy will only crush his spirit and break the bond you are trying to build; it will not correct his behavior or make the process faster.

Be patient and consistent with your potty training routine and be gentle, kind and loving with your puppy. You'd never yell at, punish or berate a baby for accidents, so don't do it to your puppy. Follow these potty training tips and in just a few weeks, your puppy will be potty trained and you can feel good about a job well done.

CHAPTER 4

REGULAR FEEDING

One of the causes of puppies being sick and having irregular potty patterns or diarrhea is the food you feed your puppy and how you feed him. It is important that you make sure you feed your puppy on a regular schedule. Depending on the age of the puppy, he will **need to eat between three and four times each day**. If you feed your puppy on a schedule, it is more likely he will need to relieve himself at the same time each day, which will make house training much easier for the both of you.

You need to feed your puppy a **high-quality food**, which is more easily digested and that means fewer messes. And, contrary to what you've been told, puppies do not need fresh water available at all times. Leaving a large amount of **fresh water** out for your puppy just means more pee to clean up. Give him water before and after he eats and offers it throughout the day. If it's a hot day you'll need to give him more if he's outside for any length of time. Use your best judgment on this. If you feel he isn't getting enough water, offer him a little more. If you have your puppy outside for some time you will need to have fresh water available at all times.

Always feed your puppy at the same time every day. This will get his digestive system on a set schedule so you'll have a better idea of when he needs to go out. And whatever you do, don't change his normal food! Decide what food you want to feed him and stick with it. Puppies can easily get diarrhea if their food is changed. Try hard not to give him tons of treats throughout the day. For now, stick with just giving him treats for messing outside. **Walk your puppy at the same time** every day, too. Puppies get used to certain things and will come to expect them at the time they are used to.

You should also make sure you are picking up the puppy's food and water bowl at least two and a half hours before going to bed. This will help ensure the puppy does not eat too close to bedtime or in the middle of the night, which will help ensure the puppy does not relieve himself in the house while everyone is asleep

Most puppies will be able to sleep for about seven hours without having to be taken outside. The puppy may, however, wake up in the middle of the night and need to relieve himself. Remain as quiet and calm as possible if this happens. First, do not turn on all of the lights in the house, but turn on as few as you can. Next, do not talk to the puppy or pet him, simply take him out, tell him to go potty, reward him when he is finished, and bring him back inside. If you talk to him, he is likely to think it is time to get up and play, which means he will not go back to sleep when you return indoors.

Puppy Nutrition

As discussed earlier in the previous chapters, puppy ownership entails a lot of care and much responsibilities. What to feed and how to do it, will be the first question that will come to your mind after bringing him home? Which food will be suitable food for your pup for the first few weeks or a month? Food with proper nutrient composition is needed for muscle development, organs, and strong bones.

However, it best recommended **to consult a veterinarian** first before embarking on any food program. With the rapid growth of the pup, there is need to keep on changing the food quality for his better health. Therefore, when it comes to feeding puppies, special care needs to be taken. It's important to ensure that certain essential nutrients are included in their diet to promote the healthy growth of bones, nervous system and coat. Due to their fragile digestive systems, try to give him the same food he ate before coming to your house. Gradually, over a one-week transition period, you can mix the old and new food.

Any food you purchase should be able to state in the labels the life stage for which the food is most suited for. If any food is labeled for "**growth**" or "**for all stages of life**", it is probably a good food choice for your puppy.

It is time to access your puppy after feeding him a particular food for 6 weeks. If he is playful and energetic with a thick shiny coat, then he is probably digesting all his nutrients and there are no causes for alarm.

Know the right way to feed the puppy

Puppies that are not 6 months old yet should be fed thrice a day. After they reach 6 months old, it is okay **to feed them twice a day**. It is important to take advantage of the feeding guides provided on the labels on the puppy food. You should vary the amount of food you give your puppy every week ensuring the puppy is in a healthy and playful condition. Puppies require a lot of calories as they are still growing. Therefore it is important to check out your puppy's expected body size when you purchase him, so as to ensure he is eating the right food for his growth.

Some largely bred dogs develop skeletal and joint problems as they grow. This caused by the lack of certain nutrients that support growth in the largely bred dogs. The conditions can worsen if the puppy is overfed. It is important to take care when purchasing puppy food and be certain that the food will be of great benefit to the puppy in terms of growth and health. Foods meant for larger breeds tend to be low in calcium but high in fiber as they are designed to control the growth of the puppy.

How to discern the right kind of food

With the ever growing dog food industry, there are unlimited varieties and alternative of food that you can choose for your puppy. There are three main dog food that is dry food, wet food and dry food that can be served wet. You can opt for the best brand or go for a generic food if you are planning on saving money. The following factors are important in helping you choose the best food for your puppy:

- ✓ **Cost** - in the market, wet food is generally more expensive than dry food. Your choice of food will depend on your budget.

- ✓ **Nutrients** - In terms of nutrition, the dry food is the best option. This is because the dry food takes a longer time to digest, unlike wet food that passes through the puppy very quickly. Wet food will not allow the puppy to absorb most of the nutrients due to the short time it takes in the digestion system of the puppy.

✓ **Storage** - Another determinant is the shelf life and storage of the dog food. Dry food is easily stored in a container with a lid. The dry food has a longer shelf life and can be stored for several months. On the other hand, wet food is hard to store and once opened it has a shorter shelf life and goes bad after a short period. Thus the storage and shelf life of the puppy food will play a big role in determining the best food for your puppy.

✓ **Dental Health** - The dental health of your puppy is determined by the food you give him. Experts recommend feeding your puppy dry food, apart from the fact that it makes it easy for potty training; dry food does not get trapped in the puppy's teeth. Wet food gets trapped in the puppy teeth and these may encourage bacterial infection causing the teeth to decay and unpleasant smell from your puppy's mouth.

It is **much healthier** for your puppy if you fed him either wet food or dry food. Avoid going for the moist food which has nutritional imbalance and high level of preservatives especially salt which may affect the health of your puppy negatively. You can also alternate between dry and wet food when feeding your puppy. For example, a meal of wet food can be followed by two meals of dry food can prove beneficial with a high amount of nutrients. However, it is advisable to ask the vet about the best combination for your puppy.

For the brand of puppy food, is good to go for **the most reputable brand** with the best nutrients for your puppy. The brand choice is also determined by the pricing and whether it is natural or generic.

CHAPTER 6

CREATING A ROUTINE

The most important step in potty training a dog is to create **a schedule**. Puppies and dogs do best when they follow a routine. Having a schedule teaches the dog that there are specific times for him to do specific activities. For example, there is a specific time for him to eat, there is a specific time each day for him to go for a walk and there are specific times each day for him to be taken outside to relieve himself. Most puppies can hold their bladder for 1 hour for every month of their age. This means that if the puppy is three months old, he can hold his bladder for three hours, however, you should never make him hold it for any amount of time longer than that.

Begin by taking your puppy outside **at least every two hours**. You will also want to take the puppy outside as soon as he wakes up in the morning, before bed at night, after play time, as well as after he has had something to eat or drink.

It is important to pick a place outside for your dog's bathroom area. This is because you do not want the dog going all over the yard, and you want to build a routine with him. Lead the dog to the area on his leash and say something like, **"Go potty."** After he has relieved himself, **give him praise**. You can also take him for a walk, or spend a few minutes playing with him to reinforce this behavior.

You can give your puppy a treat after he has relieved himself outside, but you have to remember to do this while you are still outside, and not once you have gone back into the house. You should also make sure the puppy is completely finished relieving himself before you give him the treat. This is because it is very easy for a puppy to become distracted, and if this happens, the puppy may forget he was not done and then remember once he is back inside of the house.

Daily Routine

Routine will make the puppy feel secure and will result in faster potty training. A sample daily routine looks like this and can easily be adjusted to fit any family's schedule:

7:00 am – 7:30 am

Wake up and go for a walk. Provide some playtime with the opportunity for the puppy to do his business.

7:30 am – 8:00 am

Feed the puppy breakfast in his crate. It is appropriate to feed on a Kong or other interactive item so the puppy learns to chew appropriate items, to stretch meal time out and have them eat slowly and to occupy the puppy for a period of time.

8:00 am – 9:00 am

After eating, give the puppy an outdoor opportunity to relieve himself.

9:00 am – 12:00 pm

The puppy might nap for a bit and then you can spend some time with him. You should give puppies the opportunity to do their business outside as soon as they wake up and after playtimes so they quickly learn to potty outside.

Puppy can go out for a walk with you.

Have a short (no more than 5 minutes) training session with rewards. Dogs learn quickly when they have frequent but short (less than 5 minutes) training sessions throughout the day.

12:00 pm – 1:00 pm

Take the puppy outside for a potty break, and then have a gentle playtime outside if the weather permits. Provide a meal in a Kong, puppies up to 16 weeks should have three meals a day. Then, 15 minutes after the puppy has finished eating, provide another potty opportunity outside.

1:00 pm – 5:00 pm

Give the puppy the opportunity to nap if he would like to. When he wakes, take him outside to do his business and then have a gentle playtime. Provide an opportunity for the puppy to nap again.

5:00 pm – 6:00 pm

Take the puppy outside for a break. Then take the puppy for a walk, and have a playtime and a short training session. It is important to play with your puppy as this is a bond building relationship opportunity and it creates rewards other than treats.

6:00 pm

Dinner with a Kong filled with the puppy's food or another interactive food dispensing toy.

6:15 pm or 6:30 pm

Bathroom break

7:30 pm – 10:00 pm

This is a good opportunity to brush and groom your dog, gently brush his teeth, and do quiet activities. Have a short evening walk.

Before Bedtime

Give the puppy another opportunity to go out and do their business one last time. After any activity, give the puppy an opportunity to relieve herself outside.

Remember all interactions with puppies are learning opportunities, so manage the interactions so the puppy is learning the right things and therefore enjoying learning.

CONCLUSION

It is both an amazing feeling and experience to have a well behaved energetic dog. However to achieve such a result you have to work and concentrate on your puppy so that when he grows, he is everything you expected. Potty training a puppy is one of the most difficult behavior training for a puppy owner. It takes a lot of patience and commitment to have a well potty trained puppy. So if you are thinking of getting a puppy or ready have one, get ready to get dirty when potty training him so that you can have a tidy dog in the future. Raise him like one of your own and make the bond grow stronger each day. It is important to be optimistic and slow to anger when you find or unfortunately, step on his poop or pee on. After reading this book to the last full stop, you will be able to potty train your puppy like a professional trainer and reap the benefits of having both a clean house and puppy.

GOOD LUCK!

Also see my book about Puppy Training

You can find it here
https://www.amazon.com/dp/B01NB1ED04

73954940R00022

Made in the USA
San Bernardino, CA
11 April 2018

Potty training a pup can often turn out to be a tough task. It might sometimes seem like a simple work but at the end turn out to be annoying and frustrating if done wrongly.

With little know how you will end up wasting a lot of energy and time resulting to frustrations. The Main goal of this book is to simplify and enlighten any new owner to potty training. In addition, add more knowledge to all pup owners on how to effective potty train a puppy. The book will solve all common problems you may go through during the potty training process.

Without proper potty training tricks and techniques, it may be difficult for a puppy to learn how to potty effectively. This book will showcase the best ways to train your puppy well. Remember, patience is a significant factor to consider while potty training your puppy.

As a pup owner, you expect the dog to bring a lot of happiness in the home but without the essential potty training techniques, it's going to be a bad experience between you and the puppy. Get rid of all bad experience by making this book your teacher.

ISBN 9781520862149

90000

9 781520 862149